The Southern Girl's Sweet Tea Diet
And Other Stories

A Short, and Mostly Sweet, Memoir

by Caroline Hammond Stephenson

To Beth

Ci St

TABLE OF CONTENTS

For Callie, Hal, Ali, and Keenan
The stars in my Southern sky

Chapter 1

The Southern Girl's Sweet Tea Diet

Tea: a rich honey-colored liquid, reminiscent of the smooth tannin-tinted waters of the Waccamaw River I swam in as a child during South Carolina summers at the beach. Sweetened to perfection when hot, of course, with just the precise amount of sparkling white Dixie Crystals cane sugar, so it pours out in a slow, syrupy stream. Chilled, poured over ice in a tall glass, and garnished with a tart, juicy lemon wedge.

Its simplicity is the soul of elegance, yet its taste is the nectar of the Gods.

Growing up in the South, I never knew that iced

1

tea could be anything but sweet. My mother, father, grandmother, grandfather, relatives, and friends all drank sweet tea. It was a universal beverage, served anytime of the day or night (although after 6:00 p.m., when you were of legal age, more spirited liquids were usually imbibed). Sweet tea is an appropriate choice of drink to serve at a luncheon or a barbeque. It's served in the most exclusive clubs and at the local "meat and three." Governors drink it, as do car mechanics. Sweet tea is a mainstay of Southern culture.

To offer someone a glass of this luscious liquid is a gesture of hospitality that is purely Southern. It conveys welcome, generosity, and friendship—traits a Southerner values as much as a firm handshake and good manners.

I first met my friend, Kaki Manning Zeigler, when I was ten years old, at summer camp. She grew up in the state capital of Columbia, and I in Greenville, about two hours up the road. Kaki's grandmother, Katherine Manning, had married Jim Perry, a charming Southern gent who owned Camp Sky Valley in Hendersonville, North Carolina. My mother had attended this camp as a child and I, of course, would carry on the family tradition. My friendship with Kaki has lasted over fifty years, and on a recent girls' trip to Litchfield Beach, South Carolina, Kaki made an observation which became a revelation.

As she tore open her little pink, blue, and yellow packets of artificial sweetener, she noticed all her willowy friends had ordered sweet tea. The size twos, fours, and sixes consumed mass quantities of the syrupy drink—and even got "go glasses" to take with them on their afternoon of shopping. As we purchased more size twos, fours, and sixes, Kaki was uncharacteristically quiet. Over cocktails that evening, she made an announcement: "All my friends who drink sweet tea are thin!"

This revelation prompted Kaki and me to begin our highly technical research on this subject, which involved eating lunch out every day and observing who drank what. Against all health advice and common sense, Kaki's proclamation proved to be true. Whether it was at McDonald's or Forest Lake Club, the female privates from nearby Ft. Jackson or the debutantes from The Camellia Ball, the girls with the tight abs and flat stomachs were all drinking sweet tea!

Once Kaki and I had collected enough evidence

to prove our point, we felt it would be unfair of us not to share this discovery with women everywhere. I mean, Southern girls are generally hospitable, and just think how a secret as elementary as the "sweet tea diet" could help our fellow sisters struggling with their weight.[1]

As I share with you some stories of the more interesting events of my life, perhaps you may decide that the consumption of this magic elixir may also have produced some mysterious psyche-altering qualities, reflected in my family and concentrated in my mother.

---

1. This diet should not be attempted by anyone suffering from diabetes, as it would be fatal!

Chapter 2

A Little Bit Of History

I had the good fortune of being born into a nice Southern family in Greenville, South Carolina, in the early 1950s. Even more fortunate was the fact that I had a wise and caring father and doting maternal grand-parents. Not quite as fortunate was the fact that my beautiful mother, Joanne, the offspring of the doting grandparents, was a charming but mercurial hellcat.

From the time she was a little girl, Joanne was considered precocious, which is a euphemism for trouble! Joanne lived her life "upsetting the apple cart." Never satisfied with the peaceful status quo, she tested her parents' limits of patience throughout her childhood and adolescence. She was blond, pretty, smart, and, most importantly, understood what it took to get her way.

By the time she got to high school, Joanne had honed her skills of persuasion and charm and was the belle of the ball. Even though she and my father had both attended Greenville High School, they weren't there at the same time due to their five-year age difference. The moment that changed all our lives was when "The Greenville News" ran a photo of Joanne descending the steps of an airplane as she returned to Greenville from Rollins College for Thanksgiving break. Daddy was smitten by the photograph, and even more so once he met Joanne herself. Their courtship lasted a year, followed by a wedding and lavish reception featuring Greenville's first open bar. When I arrived a year later, Joanne's destiny was set. Her ambition was to have her children and husband worship her, fear her, and take every word she spoke as the complete truth, as if Jesus Christ had descended from Heaven and uttered it himself.

My mother maintained that our family had a better pedigree than Queen Elizabeth II (who is German after all, while we are Southerners with a purely English background). She frequently reminded my brother, sister, and me that we were of aristocratic stock, meaning that we had long, narrow feet requiring very expensive shoes, a predisposition to "throw a fit," always had a better idea than anyone else, and contained the innate knowledge that it is more sophisticated to say "stockings" than "hose," along with other proper word choices. Our gentrified heritage also meant we possessed an inordinate love for dogs, could handle difficult horses, and knew how to make sweet tea. Above and beyond all of this, our venerated ancestry instilled in us an ingrained belief in our family's superiority. No one on earth, not the most famous movie star, the richest man in America, and certainly not a mere politician such as the President of the United States, could match our family credentials, she assured us.

She referred to our hometown of Greenville as the "Cradle of Western Civilization," Mesopotamia be damned! While this type of belief makes for great stories, it often caused our lives to be very turbulent. The family credo was that Momma was never happy when things were calm and peaceful. Just when we thought we had settled into a steady-paced life, she would always create some dissension to stir the pot.

My mother had a knack for altering the truth to suit her needs. This trait began at a young age and persisted throughout her life. When she was in first grade at Augusta Circle School, my grandmother was president of the PTA. In this position she was attuned to the school's curriculum and policies. When my mother arrived home after school one day, she told my grandmother that she would need to take a nickel to school the following day to purchase a Coca-Cola from the drink machine in her classroom. After an intense line of questioning from my grandmother, my mother reluctantly confessed that there was not a Coke machine in her classroom yet, but they would be getting one soon, and she wanted to be prepared.

This predisposition for falsehoods grew as she did until, as an adult, it had become a finely tuned art. If the facts didn't suit her purposes, she would repeat the lies so often, they would become her version of the truth. Once after she became a member of PETA (or claimed to be), I asked my mother, the former meat lover, if she would give me her full-length mink coat since she would no longer wear animal fur. She said she had given it to a thrift shop. After her death, my father found it hanging in the coat closet. She had the ability to rearrange the facts to suit her every need.

Joanne loved to spend money and, thankfully, my father was adept at making it. As a youth, when my father and his brother managed to get their hands on some change, my father would hatch a plan to double his money while his brother would race to the store to spend his. On one such occasion, they were each given a dime. My father went to the bakery and bought two cookies. The next day he took them to school and sold them for ten cents a piece. Meanwhile, his brother had run through his windfall and had nothing to show for it. As they grew into adults, his brother married my aunt Martha, a very frugal woman, and Daddy married my extravagant mother. This decision changed the trajectory of their lives.

My mother's first forty-five years were by far her most settled. She could be personable, involved, and often charming when she so chose, but lurking beneath this veneer, her true emotions were always simmering, just below the surface. As we age, often our predominant characteristics become even more pronounced, and this was certainly true with my mother. She always had a penchant for "bucking the norm" and letting you know in no uncertain terms how she felt. But for a while, she managed to keep these sentiments in check and fit into normal life in Greenville.

She was a member of the Junior League, chairperson of the Greenville Republican Women's Club, and although not a regular church-goer, was a member in good standing at Buncombe Street Methodist Church.

Sometime during her mid-forties, though, things began to change. Joanne traded her Ferragamo's for Birkenstocks, renounced the Republican Party and the Methodist church, and claimed to be both a Democrat and a Buddhist. She loved the shock value and attention her conversion caused among her conservative friends.

She would launch into long dissertations on the virtues of Democratic candidates, causing much dissension among their mainstream crowd. My father calmly listened to her tirades, and then went to the polls and cast his vote for the Republican ticket, along with the rest of their friends.

We were all encouraged by Joanne's switch to Buddhism, though, hoping that the calmness and serenity professed by this religious group would rub off on her and produce many "ohm" moments. But no such luck! My father even took her to an ashram in California to pray for peace, but all he got was "the worst food he'd ever eaten in his life and no alcohol."

That was when he shared with me some very sage advice. "Caroline, don't ever go anywhere without room liquor," defined as a container of your favorite spirits to partake of in your hotel room. From that day forward I always carry a flask when traveling!

Upon their return from the Buddhist retreat, my mother became even more cantankerous. Most normal people try to avoid taboo subjects, such as religion and politics, but my mother thrived on these incendiary topics and enjoyed interjecting them into conversations. It got so bad that we talked with her doctor about putting her on a mood-altering drug. He agreed, and surprisingly, she did too and took the medication. For three wonderful months, she was an absolute delight. Then, one morning my father awoke to the old combative Joanne. He asked if she had quit taking her pills and she told him, "Yes."

"Why?" he asked.

To which she replied, "Because I was Goddamn sick of being nice!"

Not "the face that launched a thousand ships," but the photo that changed our lives. My mother descending the steps of an airplane as she returned to Greenville from Rollins College for the Thanksgiving holidays.

Chapter 3

A Lesson In Parenting At An Early Age

Growing up, the beverage I consumed the most of, besides the prerequisite milk and sweet tea, was beer. You might reasonably ask why a child would drink mass quantities of an alcoholic beverage. Well, the truth is, it is a long four-hour car trip from Greenville to the beach, and my brother, sister, and I could be a little hard to handle during that extensive duration in the car. We were very concerned with our personal property lines in the back seat of our station wagon, and, if one dared to cross into the other's space, all hell would break loose.

Our parents let us have a sip of their beer on the beach and discovered we liked it. So thereafter, before each road trip, my mother would pour us a glass of beer, which we would gulp down, and then promptly fall asleep in the car, only to be awakened when we arrived at our destination. No more fighting!

One thing my parents excelled in was having a good time. With their circle of fun-loving friends, they were always cooking up some new adventure. Their merry band of revelers were forever on the lookout for an entertaining excursion, whether near or far, and they were acolytes of creativity. On some of these escapades, the children were included.

One cold Sunday morning, we awoke to a blanket of snow covering our yard. It didn't take long for our parental units to hatch a plan. They decided that if there was snow in Greenville, then the Blue Ridge Parkway outside of Asheville, North Carolina, would be knee-deep in it and the perfect place to go sledding. And, indeed, it was!

Once our fathers had put the chains on our tires to drive through the snow, we headed to the Parkway in four-wheel drive Jeeps. Upon our arrival, our parents promptly built a fire and began to "toast" the snow with adult beverages. As the two oldest children among their social crowd, my childhood friend, Edwin Haskell and I, were usually given the task of supervising our younger siblings—a job neither of us relished. Edwin and I unloaded the sleds, and all the children would streak down the parkway for miles. When they reached the bottom of the mountain, Edwin and I would take turns pulling the younger children back up the mountain, behind a Jeep that was used to navigate the snow-covered Parkway.

We were the least of our parents' concerns. They were just happy to have two built-in babysitters!

On another wintry day, they bundled us up, and we took off for Highlands, North Carolina, to ice skate on Mirror Lake. We had a ball skating, and they had an equally good time drinking hot toddies around the bonfire.

My parents, like most of their generation who had grown up during the Depression, were loath to throw anything away. We had an endless supply of margarine tubs, pre-used plastic bags, and antiquated Styrofoam cups from every restaurant in town. But overshadowing all these relics were the contents of their refrigerator. To open the door of that large appliance was to take a step back into the Prehistoric Age of food items.

One particular Saturday evening after a Clemson-Georgia Tech football game, my parents were entertaining their friends at our house. One of their buddies, who had grown up in Greenville but now resided in the cosmopolitan city of Atlanta, requested my father mix him a martini. This aperitif was considered quite exotic at the time in Greenville, where bourbon and water and vodka tonics were de rigueur. While tending the bar, my father instructed me to go to the refrigerator and bring him some olives for the martini.

Upon opening the door, I espied a jar of olives in the back corner of the top shelf whose label read "Green Olives Stuffed with Red Pimento." However, the contents of the jar revealed what appeared to be black ripe olives. I brought the jar to my father, who nodded his approval. I surmised that this would be the first martini ever to be garnished with ripe olives. Then to my horror, my father dug two of the black orbs out of the jar and ran them under some hot water. When the black mold was washed away, two red and green olives miraculously appeared. I implored my father not to put those olives in the martini. He looked at me and said simply, "Of course I will. They've been in the refrigerator and anything a little hot water won't wash away, the gin will kill."

This may explain why today the interior of my refrigerator looks like that of a display model at the appliance store: very sparsely stocked!

THE IMPORTANT 3

IN COLLEGE

SWEATER FASHION

The sweater to be worn
—the turtle neck in
sleeves 5.95. Rust, grey,
yellow, green. 34 to 40

All wool Cashmeres in soft
pastel shades and new rich
fall colors. Short sleeve pull-
over 15.95. Cardigan 19.95. 34
to 40 sizes.

Our newest waffle-stitch
sleeveless sweater 5.95. Yellow, red, green, royal blue.
34 to 40 sizes.

My mother, Joanne, (far left) in a fall photo shoot during her college
years

Chapter 4

The Family Tree

My maternal grandparents played a major role in my life. Living less than a mile up the mountain from our house, I could escape my mother's mood swings by riding my bicycle up to the sanctuary of my grandparents' house, where open arms and loving hugs awaited. My grandfather taught me to play gin rummy, pick scuppernongs, and whistle. My grandmother made me dress-up costumes, turned her upstairs bedroom into my playroom, and taught me to knit and cook. Somehow, whereas my grandparents had failed in raising their own children, the lessons they taught me were some of the most valuable of my life.

One particular trying time for me was during my divorce from my first husband. I was in tears when I told my mother of his dirty deeds, hoping for sympathy and understanding. She merely peered at me over her reading glasses and said I had gotten rid of the one minus in my life. She went on to say that I needed to handle it in the manner of Erica Kane, the star of the soap opera *All My Children*, who had been divorced ten times. She then returned to her book, totally dismissing me and my problem.

Luckily for me, I had wonderful support from my father and grandmother. During this time of despair, I became very thin. It was the syndrome I now dub the "divorce diet." In times of upheaval, many people either are either unable even to look at food or tend to overindulge. I was in the former category. I had lost twelve pounds and was still headed south on the scale. My compassionate father was very concerned about my wasting away. As we were eating lunch together one day, he told me a story which he hoped would stimulate my desire for food. As he studied my ultra-thin frame, he told me, "Caroline, I've been around a lot of men in my life who have had preferences for different types of women's figures. I've known leg men, fanny men, and breast men, but I've never known a bone man in my life!" This statement had the desired effect on me, as I promptly summoned the waiter and ordered a hot fudge sundae.

I also thank the Lord for my darling grandmother who nurtured me through this difficult time. One weekend during my divorce, my children and I were in Greenville spending the weekend with her. After church on Sunday, she took us to the Greenville Country Club for lunch. As I watched all the happy, nuclear families move through the buffet line, I became more and more morose. Sensing my sadness, my grandmother told me to look at the family that had just entered the dining room. There they were— the mother, father, and two handsome children—the picture of the perfect family.

"Things are not always as they seem," my grandmother said.

I peered at her quizzically. Well, as it so happened the husband had just been busted in Operation Lost Trust, South Carolina's largest and longest-running political scandal. The family was making a very public show of unity, but there was trouble in paradise.

My problems didn't seem so large anymore. My grandmother went on to tell me that once my divorce was over, living well is the best revenge.

I am now married to a wonderful man and have two accomplished grown children and wonderful lifelong friends. I wake up every morning grateful to live on the sunny side of the street, realizing the truth of my grandmother's statement. Cheers!

Chapter 5

The Chapel Cap

My parents sent my siblings and me to Christ Church Episcopal School in Greenville. All students, regardless of their personal denominations, were required to attend chapel daily. The Episcopalians back then believed that young ladies should cover their heads in chapel with a skimpy piece of lace called a chapel cap. These "caps" could be purchased at Ivey's department store on Main Street and cost $3.00. Although our parents gave us a small allowance, this was perceived by my sister and me to be a huge sum of money that could be better spent on candy and comic books. So rather than buying a chapel cap, we rode our bicycles to the local drug store and stocked up on M&Ms and Snickers. The end result of this folly was that I was issued the dreaded "Thursday card" from my teacher for not wearing a chapel cap to church. At CCES, the worst chastisement you could receive for the most grievous offense was a note to your parents known as the "Thursday card." It covered all forms of violations of school policy and when issued, sent fear through the heart of the offender, who dreaded the ordeal of presenting it to their parents for their signature before returning it to the teacher.

I arrived home that Thursday with a huge sense of foreboding, with the "Thursday card" feeling like an anvil in my book bag. My mother's bridge club was just finishing up their afternoon of cards, and once they had said their goodbyes, I knew it was time to confess my sin. As I had been raised a good Methodist, I thought it might be in my best interest to feign ignorance about the importance of a chapel cap. This proved to be a sage tactic. As my mother read the "Thursday card," I could tell she was not happy. Luckily for me, her anger was directed at the Episcopalians and not at her wayward child. Instead of simply signing the "Thursday card," she went to her desk and began furiously writing a comment back to my teacher. The message was as follows:

"My daughter is a good Methodist and, as such, does not require a piece of cloth on her head to enter church. All she is required to have upon entering the house of the Lord is a prayerful heart. If you would like to discuss this with me, I welcome the opportunity because I am certain I can quote more scripture than you!"

From that day on, my sister and I were the only two girls in the entire school allowed to attend chapel with a bare head.

Chapter 6

Sunday Traditions

Sundays are a day of rituals in the South. Ours started when we heard our father's voice crackle through the intercoms in each of our bedrooms giving us the wake-up call. We'd dress in our best church clothes and eat a hearty breakfast of eggs, bacon, grits, and pancakes cooked by my father, but here's where our similarities with other families ceased.

You need a little family history to understand the situation and how it relates to our Sundays. My mother was quite an athlete—the club tennis champion, in fact—but to become this adept at a sport requires a lot of time practicing and taking lessons.

In turn, this necessitates having someone watch your children during your absences. Our household was in dire straits as our housekeeper, who had previously been the cook, the cleaner, and the child-minder in our house, had recently quit to move to Detroit. So our mother was now housebound to look after us, but the laundry was piling up and we were eating a lot of TV dinners. One afternoon, her tennis friend, Frankie Eppes, whose husband was a semi-famous circuit court judge as well as being my future husband's godfather, phoned. It seemed Frankie's husband had a problem that would turn into a win-win situation for my mother.

Judge Eppes had presided over a parole hearing for a woman who had, in the heat of passion and with the assistance of another woman, killed a man. The judge was a compassionate man and felt the killing had simply been a crime of passion and was certain Alberta would never kill again. He wanted to approve her parole, but there was one caveat: she couldn't be released from prison without having a job. Frankie instantly thought of my mother and her three small children who were in desperate need of help.

My mother didn't hesitate even a nano-second before hiring Alberta, the convicted killer, to care for us. One Monday morning, Alberta showed up at our door with a long scar from her ear to her chin that she had sustained in the knife fight. We children were instantly charmed and adored her. She had a hilarious sense of humor and entertained the three of us with colorful stories about her stints in prison. She took us for long walks, where we discovered crawfish and salamanders. And she made the most delicious biscuits. There was just one small problem. Every Saturday night she would go honky-tonking and get rip-roaring drunk, which would result in her being incarcerated in the Greenville Police Department jail.

So, getting back to Sunday mornings, my daddy would take the three of us to Sunday School, as we dared not wake our mother from her peaceful slumber. Following Sunday School, we would head to church, where Daddy was an usher. As soon as the collection plates were returned to the altar, the three of us and our father would skip the sermon and head to jail to pick up Alberta, who was still reeking of stale alcohol. Upon depositing her at her home in Happy Hearts Park, where she'd sleep it off, we'd return to our house to pick up our mother, who was not a fan of organized religion, and head to the country club for lunch. Ahh, the sweet memories of Sundays in the South.

Chapter 7

The Airplane

Once we children were tucked into bed at night, we didn't lay eyes on our mother until after school the next day. Let's just say that she wasn't a morning person; it was better to let sleeping dogs lie! Daddy cooked us breakfast, made sure we'd brushed our teeth, got our lunches together, and took us to school.

Once I turned fifteen and went to high school, I inherited my mother's old Valiant station wagon and achieved a much desired level of freedom. I was out of the house by 8:00 a.m. and didn't return until late afternoon. The soda jerk at Campbell's Pharmacy, our favorite hangout, was a friend of mine. In fact, we had grown up in the same Methodist Sunday school class until he was held back one year for some innocent little pranks. Until that time, I had never met anyone who had flunked Sunday School.

One afternoon while sipping a cherry Coke at Campbell's, the soda jerk told me he was taking flying lessons at the downtown airport and invited me to accompany him on his first solo flight. I jumped at the opportunity, as I had never before ridden in an airplane. When he asked where I wanted to go, I suggested we fly over and buzz my parents' home. In the little single-engine plane, we would swoop down low in a daring dip, the motor humming, just missing the roof of their house. This practice went on every day for a week, until one night at the dinner table, my mother mentioned to my father that a small plane had been swooping down very low over our house for the past week. Proudly, I let them know that the aviators were the soda jerk and me.

Big mistake! They were horrified at me for taking this risk and pulling a prank on them. From that moment forward, I was forbidden to return to the friendly skies until I flew on Piedmont Airlines to attend Rollins College.

That night was when I learned the value of remaining silent!

Chapter 8

For The Birds

One Saturday morning in high school, I was sleeping peacefully when I was suddenly awakened by a gunshot outside my window. I jumped out of bed and ran downstairs to my parents' bedroom, which was below mine. That's where I found my mother on her balcony with a smoking shotgun in her hand. Not twenty feet from her lay what remained of a dead mockingbird. In stunned horror, I stared at her and said in the words of Harper Lee, "Momma, it's a sin to kill a mockingbird."

She turned, replaced her sleep mask, crawled

back into bed, and said, "Not when it interferes with my beauty sleep!"

While I felt badly for the poor dead mockingbird, I've never been a fan of birds ever since an incident that occurred when I was in sixth grade. One of my classmates had invited me to a sleepover on a Friday night. As we were in her bedroom changing into our pajamas, she decided to let her two parakeets out of their cage. The green one made a bee line for me and became tangled in my hair, fluttering furiously. I finally had to dive under her bed to get him off me and spent the remainder of the night washing bird poop out of my hair.

That experience scarred me for life. Other than sharks and snakes, there is no creature on earth more fearsome to me than a free-roaming bird!

Chapter 9

Seen And Not Heard

As the oldest child, my siblings always accused me of having used up all our mother's maternal instincts. I assured them that I had not been the lucky recipient of anything that resembled nurturing. She must have exhausted her supply on the cocker spaniels she had as a child.

In the 60's and 70's, we children were not the center of our parents' world. They fed us, clothed us, educated and loved us, but we were on our own for a large part of the day. During these hours, they didn't have a clue what we were up to.

After completing ninth grade at Christ Church Episcopal School, I attended Greenville High along with my life-long friend and best buddy, Libby Knight Borders. We had both excelled in Latin at CCES, fortunate to have had a Latin scholar as our teacher. At GHS, let's just say, it was quite a different story. We had a dear old spinster, Miss Martha Frances Morgan, as our teacher. After *amo, amas, amat* and *veni, vidi, vici,* the most important thing in Miss Morgan's world of academia was for one of her students to bring home the grand prize from the annual Roman Forum held at Winthrop College in Rock Hill, South Carolina, about a two-hour drive from Greenville.

Libby and I, seeking A's in Latin, volunteered to enter the contest. I was selected to play the role of Daphne. In case your memory is a little fuzzy on Roman mythology, Daphne, fleeing to escape Apollo's advances, prays to Zeus for help. Dear old Zeus responds by turning her into a laurel tree. Libby and I stayed up until 4:00 in the morning the night before the Forum, cutting laurel leaves out of construction paper, adding glitter and stapling them onto an old dress. Bleary eyed from lack of sleep and having absolutely no idea how to get to Rock Hill, we hit the road at 6:00 a.m. with my newly minted driver's license. There wasn't an interstate in those days, but by some miracle, with St. Christopher guiding us, we made it to Winthrop and brought home the prize for Miss Morgan and dear old GHS!

When I arrived at my parents' home around dusk, my mother asked what I had been doing all day. I regaled her about my 12-hour odyssey, hoping for some parental concern, but she feigned complete nonchalance, stating that any fifteen-year-old should be able to find her way to Rock Hill and back! Yes, my mother was definitely missing some maternal feelings.

My mother posing for a fall fashion feature in The
Greenville News

Chapter 10

The Pot

My sister, brother, and I continued the family tradition of attending and graduating from Clemson University, located in South Carolina's beautiful foothills. As the oldest child in our family, my mother was much younger than many of my friends' parents, having given birth to me when she was just 21 years old. Perhaps due to her youth and good looks, she always wanted to be involved in whatever was "in" at the moment—whether it was miniskirts, Sperry Topsiders, or the Rolling Stones. But, more than anything, she was dying to try marijuana. She would hike through our pastures, picking vegetation hoping it would be the evil weed, but no such luck! She spoke about it freely to anyone who would listen—my dad, her tennis partner, the yard man, the bridge club, and most importantly, Bobbie, the cashier at the Winn-Dixie.

During my senior year at Clemson, in 1975, I was sitting in my dorm room studying Shakespeare when the wall phone rang. It was my mother, and she was so excited I could hardly understand her. Once she calmed down, she instructed me to go to the college library and check out a book on harvesting marijuana and come home immediately. Still in a state of shock, but being the obedient eldest child, I did as I was told. Upon arriving at my parents' house an hour later, I was stunned to discover that my father had grown a bumper crop of marijuana in his vegetable garden!

I was appalled that my father, a good law-abiding citizen and pillar of the community, would do such a thing. It turns out that Bobbie, the cashier at Winn-Dixie, had a role to play here—she had slipped a joint into her Christmas card to my mother! After thoughtful consideration, my mother had unrolled the joint, extracted the seeds, and in the spring, when Daddy was tilling the soil for his garden, presented the seeds to him, proclaiming them to be a new strain of okra developed by Clemson University! The garden began to grow, but the marijuana plants were far outpacing the tomatoes, squash, and cucumbers. So much so that one afternoon after returning from his garden, my father proudly exclaimed to my mother that the new okra was "growing like a weed!"

By the time all was said and done, we had harvested so much pot it filled three gigantic shopping bags. My parents gave little bags of it to their friends at Christmas, much to the chagrin of many of them. For anyone who wanted any, it was there for the taking, until my sister went to graduate school and the marijuana mysteriously disappeared at the exact same time my sister's wardrobe dramatically improved.

The irony of the entire escapade was my mother swore she never smoked even one puff, as she preferred vodka as her drug of choice.

Chapter 11

The Weight Loss

My mother was a real beauty. Tall and blond with long, slender legs. My father liked to say that 90% of the time, she got by on her looks. Her mantra was, "You can never be too rich, too thin, or too blond." This adage proved to be true most of her adult life, except for a brief period when she gained forty pounds after giving up cigarettes.

It drove her mother and my grandmother, for whom I am named, crazy that Mom had "let herself go." My grandmother, who was a champion of the practice of self-control, devised all kinds of plans to get my mother to lose weight.

Her first idea was an intervention involving her, my sister, my mother, and myself. The venue we chose for this intervention, a restaurant specializing in homemade desserts, was in hindsight a big mistake. My mother had consumed a cheeseburger and French fries and was salivating over a piece of chocolate cake when I chose to begin the intervention. I looked earnestly at my mother and began, "Momma, you've always been so pretty…"

But before I was able to say another word, she told me, "Quit beating around the bush and get to the point."

"Okay," I said. "Those extra forty pounds aren't doing you any favors."

Before I could go on, she cut me off and told me, "That observation doesn't mean much coming from a bag of bones like you, who is merely a hanger upon which to hang clothes!"

Her statement had the desired effect of shutting me up, but I was hoping my sister and grandmother would continue the intervention. However, after witnessing my mother's reaction, it seemed they had been struck dumb. At this point and without any further conversation, we piled in the car, and

Momma ate her cake on the trip home.

Another idea my grandmother had was to send my mother to Structure House, a renowned weight-loss clinic at Duke University. This was the 1980s, and it cost $1000 a week to be a client at Structure House. My mother agreed to go, and upon arrival, she immediately recognized that she was the cutest, thinnest person there. She reveled in her three weeks there, during which time she lost three pounds or, in other words, $1000 per pound!

Momma finally decided on her own to lose the weight. I think she figured out that being plump was not conducive to getting the attention she desired. As her pounds disappeared, her good looks returned, but unfortunately were not matched by a good disposition. That part of the equation was filled by my father.

My parents at Buncombe Street Methodist Church

Chapter 12

New Year's Eve

The date was December 31, 1981. The setting—The Litchfield Country Club. The participants—my parents and their friends. The moral? Oh yes, there is a moral to this story.

For those of you who don't have an encyclopedic knowledge of college football in the South, I'll give you a quick historical review. The University of Georgia Bulldogs, a fierce rival of our beloved Clemson Tigers, had won the 1980 college football national championship. The outcome of the January 1, 1982, Orange Bowl between Clemson and Nebraska would determine the 1981 college football champion.

While I, along with hordes of other orange-tiger-paw-clad fans, had driven, flown, or taken the train to Miami to watch the big game, my parents had chosen a more sedate location to spend their New Year's Eve—a country club dance. At the dance, as the clock neared midnight, my mother approached the band leader and requested that he play "Tiger Rag" for the number one team in the nation. Scarcely giving my mother a second glance, he informed her if she wanted to hear the song for the number one team in the nation he was going to play "Glory, Glory to Old Georgia" as Georgia was actually still the national champion for the next twenty-four hours.

After only a moment's hesitation, my mother gave the band leader her sweetest smile and told him, "Fuck you!" At which point he turned to the band and struck up "Tiger Rag," which he played over and over again. As my mother later related this story to me, she looked me straight in the eyes and said, "Caroline, do you understand the moral to this story?"

I stared blankly at her with a mixture of surprise and shock, dumbstruck.

"The moral is, 'Save that word until you really need it!'"

Having adopted my mother's policy regarding profanity, I must admit that once again she was right. When used seldomly, the "F" word certainly packs a bigger punch!

Chapter 13

Thanksgiving

Of the many Thanksgivings celebrated in my parents' home, one stands out. Our family was gathered around the dining room table, the linen freshly starched, the silver polished, the iced tea poured. The time for the blessing was upon us. As my father bowed his head to begin the blessing, my mother tapped her spoon on her glass and issued an edict:

"The person seated at the head of the table should have the honor of saying grace."

All fifteen heads around the table immediately shot up from our prayerful positions and fixed our eyes upon our parents. My father, calmly and diplomatically, stated that he was sitting at the head of the table, as he had done for the past thirty years. To which my mother responded that she had reassigned the head of the table, and he was now seated at the foot!

Pandemonium broke out, objections were raised by all present, the blessing was forgotten, and the tea-drinking quickly progressed to stronger beverages.

One Thanksgiving a few years later, my father suggested we share something in our lives that we were thankful for. Various family members mentioned good health, a prosperous year, the beautiful day, all with heads bowed in reverence… until it was my mother's turn. In a particularly pious voice, she said that she was eternally grateful to God that a certain cock-eyed, bubble-butted, cheating, lying skunk who was no longer a member of our family was out of our lives forever, banned to eternal exile, and preferably Hell! We all knew of whom she was referring and said "Amen!" in unison.

Chapter 14

The Rock

When my parents had been married for 30 years, my father surprised my mother with a four-and-a-half-carat diamond ring and a Greek Isles cruise aboard the Sea Cloud, which was Marjorie Merriweather Post and E. F. Hutton's former sailing yacht. Momma was delighted with her new ring and wasn't about to leave it behind in lieu of some fake "paste" while she cruised the Mediterranean on the Sea Cloud.

The first night at dinner, my parents were seated with a nice couple from Tennessee. During hors d'oeuvres as the two couples were getting to know each other, the woman from Tennessee admired my mother's ring and commented, "My, your ring is so pretty. My husband wouldn't let me bring my big ring on this trip."

Without missing a beat, my mother smiled sweetly at her and said, "Neither would mine!"

She was always quick with a comeback, and this may have been her finest hour!

Chapter 15

The Chicken Story

Every summer my family would pack up and leave Greenville and head to Litchfield Beach. As my siblings and I grew older, graduated from college, and became part of the work force, we were unable to spend our entire summers at the beach anymore. However, this did not stop my mother, who had never held a paying job in her life, from her summer sojourn at the shore. She liked to tell people that the last time she had worked was on January 18, 1932, when she descended through the birth canal!

Perceiving herself as a thoughtful wife, prior to

her departure from Greenville for the beach, she would venture into the local Winn-Dixie and stock up on food for our housekeeper, Ella, who had replaced Alberta, to cook for our father during her absence. My mother purchased, among other things, a chicken for Ella to fry. When she returned a week later and asked Ella if my father had enjoyed the chicken, Ella replied that when she got to our house on Monday, only two days after my mother had bought the chicken, it was rancid. Since grocery shopping was on my mother's "to do" list that day, she went straight to the meat counter and began pressing the buzzer to summon Charles, the butcher. As Charles was making his way to the front of the meat department, my mother noticed a man from "up North" perusing the meats. When Charles arrived, my mother explained Ella's dilemma about the rancid chicken, at which time, and much to his future dismay I'm sure, the Yankee man informed my mother that everyone knows you need to cook chicken on the day you buy it.

My mother had a wilting stare, which she gave him the full benefit of as she rose to her entire 5'9" height, looked down at him and said, "CHICKEN! CHICKEN! What do you know about chicken, you Yankee! I grew up with chickens in my yard [which she most assuredly did not!], and I know everything there is to know about chickens!"

Upon relating this story to me, I questioned my mother about the outcome of this very public put-down. She smiled sweetly and said that the Yankee left the store, and Charles gave her a free package of chicken! My mother then walked to her car, in a complete state of bliss, feeling she had righted a grievous wrong by putting that damn Yankee in his place.

Chapter 16

The Chameleon Chanteuse

My mother had always loved to sing, and when she got over-served, if there was a piano in sight, she'd belt out a few tunes. One such occasion occurred on a trip my parents took to Ireland. They were staying in an old castle that had been converted into a luxury hotel. One night after dinner and many Irish whiskeys, my parents strolled into the piano bar. It wasn't long before my mother seized the microphone and was entertaining the other guests with some of her favorite songs.

The next morning, on the elevator headed down

to breakfast, she wasn't feeling quite as chipper as she had the night before. The elevator stopped to pick up some other passengers, one of which was a couple who had been at the bar the previous evening. They, of course, immediately recognized my mother, as she was hard to miss, and told her how much they had enjoyed her singing the night before. She rolled her big blue eyes and looked pleadingly at my father, who didn't miss a beat as he turned to the couple and said, "This is my wife, Jo, but she has a crazy twin sister, Anne, [as in Jo-Anne!] who is bad to take drunk and perform in public. She must have been up to her old tricks last night!" Just one more occasion when my father saved the day!

Chapter 17

The Buick

When my father finally finished paying college tuition for the three of us, he decided to treat himself to a new car. He went to the local Buick dealership and picked out a brand new, top of the line, loaded Park Avenue. However, he made one big mistake. The color he chose was garnet—the color of the University of South Carolina—Clemson's in-state rival. When he arrived home behind the wheel of his new automobile, my mother stormed out of the house and questioned his sanity for choosing a car that color. She refused to ever put her foot in it and insisted they take her Roadmaster everywhere.

That year, my father happened to be the chairman of the building committee at the Methodist church. He and his roofing contractor were atop the church inspecting a leak when the contractor asked my father if he had a new Buick Park Avenue. Despite my mother's disapproval, he was still fond of the car, and smiling proudly, said yes, he did. Why?

The contractor, peering over the roof of the church, pointed to the street below and said, "Mr. Hammond, I think someone has stolen your car and is driving it down the street." My father looked on helplessly as the car thieves drove away. Having no transportation, he phoned my mother for a ride and explained the situation to her. She gleefully responded, "Thank God! My prayers have been answered!"

The Park Avenue was found a week later, stripped and burnt to a crisp. My father went to Collins Cadillac and bought a nice navy blue sedan. All was right in my mother's world, at least for the time being.

Chapter 18

The Police Pour Deux

My mother believed in freedom of speech and would stretch her first amendment rights to the limit. It didn't matter who you were, if you hit a nerve, she would let you have it.

I moved to Columbia after college, and my mother planned a trip to visit me with the main purpose being to purchase shoes and fabric. I was to be her personal shopper for the day. About the time she was to arrive, I heard a huge commotion in my driveway. When I opened the door, I saw blue lights streaming and my mother involved in a heated discussion with a police officer. Being loyal Clemson fans, our family gives with the regularity of a tithe to the Clemson Tigers' booster organization, which is called IPTAY.[2] My mother took great pride in stacking the past ten years' IPTAY stickers on the rear window of her Roadmaster. Also Columbia happens to be the home of the University of South Carolina, Clemson's arch rival.

As I approached the officer, I heard him tell my mother that he had been following her for over a mile, during which time she had failed to come to a complete stop at a stop sign, was speeding, ran through a yellow light, and refused to stop when he turned on his blue light. Quite a list of offenses!

Indignant, she looked at me and said, "This officer pulled me over because I'm a Clemson fan in enemy territory. Take care of it, Caroline." She then turned and strode into the house, leaving me to deal with the officer.

Thankfully, sensing my predicament, he shook his head, turned off his blue lights and said, "Good luck. You're gonna need it." Truer words had never been spoken.

---

2. IPTAY stands for "I Pay Ten a Year," the original yearly membership cost (now higher). It is one of the most successful athletic fundraising organizations in the country.

The members of my family all were born with a love for speed, cars, and the notion that driving should be an adventure, not merely a way to get you from Point A to Point B. My grandmother loved cars and always drove a Lincoln. When she was in her eighties, a drive with her at the wheel would scare the living daylights out of any passenger, due to miles of hitting curbs and swerving toward the center line. It was during this time that I discovered what that handle above the car door is for and hung on tight! In her late eighties, when her arthritis worsened, she managed to get a handicapped sticker from the DMV. Her car excursions became fewer but no less harrowing for the passenger.

One hot summer day, she realized she was almost out of vodka, so a jaunt to the liquor store was on her "to-do" list. She drove the Lincoln to her favorite liquor store, made her purchase, and as she was backing out, backed right into another old woman's car that also displayed a handicapped sticker. The Greenville Police Department was summoned, as was my father. When Daddy arrived at the liquor store, he found my grandmother lecturing the officer. She instructed the officer to get her vodka out of her car and to turn his car air conditioner off because he was using her tax dollars to run it. The officer obeyed her orders and patiently continued to listen to her. He was both grateful and relieved to deliver her to my father, who took her and her vodka home. After that episode, she never drove again, although it always gave her a sense of well-being to look out the window and see her Lincoln parked in the driveway.

Chapter 19

The Banana

My mother preferred to remain in a horizontal position every morning until my father served her breakfast in bed. Each morning, he lovingly prepared her special steel-cut oatmeal, a cup of coffee just to her liking, and a half a banana.

I think perhaps the phrase "getting up on the wrong side of the bed" was invented for my mother and was on full display one morning. As my father gently woke her and placed her breakfast tray before her, she sleepily looked it over. Then, without any gratitude whatsoever, she glared at my father and said, "Dammit to hell, Frank! You've given me the bad end of the banana!"

Until that moment, no one in our family had known that a banana had a "bad end," but to this day, we all prefer the end with the stem, which my mother had declared was the good end!

Chapter 20

Be Young, Be Foolish, Be Happy

Before I left for my freshman year of college at Rollins, a college that resembled a country club in Winter Park, Florida, which my mother had attended, my father wanted to make sure I was prepared for the nine-hour drive. The first thing he did was enroll me in AAA. Next, he gave me a corkscrew and instructed me to keep it in my glove compartment at all times, unless in use, of course. His mantra was to never get caught without a corkscrew! And the third thing was to make sure I knew how to change a tire.

So one hot August afternoon after returning home

from work, he told me to come outside so he could teach me how to perform this chore. I told my father I already knew how to change a tire. He stared at me incredulously and asked me to show him. I walked out to my white Buick Regal in my Lilly Pulitzer-print-scalloped-edge short-shorts, popped the hood, and leaned against the door. I said, "Daddy, this is all I need to do. Some guy will pull over and change my tire for me!" He shook his head, wiped his brow, and headed back into the house for a cool drink.

When I attended Rollins, academics were not at the top of my agenda. I was interested in warm weather, water skiing, tennis, and cute boys. My dream had always been to go to Clemson, my father's alma mater, but my mother insisted I first "broaden my scope" by attending college outside the state of South Carolina. After two years at Rollins, I had achieved all my goals. I had twenty hours of college credit for water skiing and tennis under my belt, had managed to have a year-round tan, which eliminated my need for stockings, and had dated many boys from chic northern prep schools. I was ready to move on and up to Clemson University. While Clemson only accepted two hours of transfer credit for my water skiing and tennis, and I actually had to study, I had landed where I was meant to be.

Every day was a new adventure! There were football games complete with carnation corsages, homecoming floats, hiking, sailing, and great Southern boys. My college beau was perfect boyfriend material—entertaining, witty, creative, a sharp dresser, and tons of fun.

After Christmas break, but before classes started in January 1974, my boyfriend heard that The Tams, a fabled beach music band, would be performing in Underground Atlanta, a hip night spot consisting of bars and restaurants. Even though it was freezing outside, he told me to wear a summer sun dress, and he would be in seersucker pants and sockless. He and his best friend picked up his date and me at our dorm at 4:00 p.m. The plan was to drive the hour and a half to Atlanta, listen to The Tams, shag awhile, and head back to Clemson later that night. Well, you know the old adage, "the best laid plans …" yada, yada, yada. In fact, the evening had been progressing according to plan until we returned to our car around midnight and found our friends waiting for us. While in Underground, they had their pictures taken at a photo booth in vintage Southern outfits. I was dying to have my picture taken in those get-ups, so my boyfriend and I headed back into Underground to find the photo booth.

Unfortunately, we were sidetracked by a bar called Scarlett O'Hara's, which had a $1.00 drink special. We quickly forgot about the photos (and our friends) and joined up with a rowdy crowd from Sewanee, with whom we partied until the wee hours of the night. We then caught a ride with them to a fraternity house at Georgia Tech, where they were staying, and all fell asleep in our individual bunk beds. When I awoke early the next morning in the cold, harsh light of dawn, I realized that we had abandoned our Clemson friends, and we had the keys to the car. I woke up my boyfriend, and we exited the frat house immediately and left to head back to our car to see what had become of our friends.

Picture this: two college kids in summer clothes in the middle of winter, hitchhiking through rush hour traffic in downtown Atlanta. That would be us! A nice businessman picked us up and dropped us off at our car, where we found a note from our friends. They had called the president of the fraternity at 2:00 a.m., and he had driven to Atlanta to retrieve them. In the note, they wished us well and said they'd see us back in Clemson. At that point, my boyfriend looked at me and said, "Well, we've got the whole day to explore Atlanta. Let's take advantage of it!" Since the previous evening I had broken a heel off my Pappagallo sandals, my boyfriend declared the first order of business would be to go to Neiman-Marcus and get me a new pair of shoes. After I was stylishly shod, we went to brunch at the famous New Orleans restaurant, Brennan's, which had a café in Atlanta. We drank Bloody Marys, ate crab Benedict, and strolled through Buckhead before finally heading back to Clemson.

Little did we know that our friends, worried sick about us, had called all the hospitals, the morgue and, worst of all, our parents! When we arrived back at the fraternity house, both sets of parents were waiting for us. All our memories of fun instantly vanished when we saw the looks on their faces. We were grilled, lectured, and threatened. We showed true remorse and hung our heads in shame. But as typical college students, we adhered to the policy, "Out of sight, out of mind," and as our parents drove out of the parking lot, we were already planning our next escapade!

It was only a few months after the Atlanta folly that I graduated from Clemson. This was in the mid 1970s at the height of the recession; jobs were hard to come by. Luckily, I had a friend in Columbia who lived in an apartment with three other girls, one of whom was to be married soon. My friend called and wanted me to come to Columbia and interview for the bride-to-be's current job. I was hired by her former employer and set to move into her old bedroom in the apartment later that week.

Unlike the children of today, we weren't set up by our parents in a fully furnished, beautifully decorated post-college residence, but most of my friends' parents at least bought them a mattress and a few pots and pans. Not mine. When it came time to leave my childhood home, my mother yelled to me as I was headed to my car. She had a frozen filet which she bestowed upon me as a parting gift. With a cocktail in one hand and a cigarette in the other, she bade me farewell and informed me I was now a member of the working class, a caste to which she had never belonged.

Chapter 21

The Lost Art Of Letter Writing

As a child, I grew up writing letters, mostly as thank-you notes for Christmas and birthday gifts. This was a dreaded task, and I sometimes wondered if receiving the present was even worth having to write the thank-you note. However, this habit led me, in part, to major in English and to continue to write today. I not only learned to love to write letters, but the anticipation of receiving a return letter was thrilling. Whether it was hearing my name at camp mail call, opening the post office box at the college post office, or running to the mailbox to see if I'd received a letter from my college boyfriend during summer break, letters were magical to me.

I've always loved telling a story, and letter writing became a way of communicating with others my thoughts and escapades at the time. Of course, every good story needs a little embellishment to make it more entertaining, and I wasn't shy about taking artistic liberties. What began as a childhood chore evolved into a pleasurable means of letting my friends in on what was happening in my life. I went into great detail about my dates, breaking curfew, the parties and after-parties I attended. However, much to my chagrin, my friends saved all the letters I had sent them during college and entertained the guests at my first wedding's rehearsal dinner by reading some of the choicer passages!

After that incident, my letter writing became a much rarer means of communication and for years, with the advent of cell phones and free long distance, I simply called friends and family. However, my mother, as she aged, had developed the bad habit of interjecting cutting remarks into a telephone conversation. She always knew where to hit you where it hurt the most, ferreting out your soft spot just like a heat-seeking missile.

One incident occurred on a Monday morning when I called to talk with her about her weekend activities. She told an elaborate story about how my siblings, their families, and dogs had spent Sunday afternoon out at the mountain with her and Daddy. She regaled me about all the fun they had. She went on to tell me she loved all their dogs (all Labs), but couldn't stand my dog (also a Lab).

I called my father in tears. He told me that the entire story had been concocted by my mother, who knew it would hurt me. From that time forward, I wrote to her weekly but rarely phoned.

One of the beautiful features of writing a letter is you control the content, form, and tone. All this is done from a distance, so there can be no stinging retorts. If you try to learn something from not only the positive but also the negative events in your life, I have my mother to thank for my continuing love of the lost art of letter writing and the pleasure I derive from putting pen to paper.

Chapter 22

The "WC"

Dubbed the "Wonder Child" by my sister and me, my brother Frank had the unique ability to get our mother to agree to his every wish. You may think this would have spoiled him, but it merely gave him the confidence to live life on his own terms. His best friends are still his childhood buddies, he has a urinal on the wall in his master bath, and he placed a full-size picture of Ronald Reagan over the mantle in his lake house, which also features an outboard motor for a mailbox. My sister-in-law is a saint!

❖ ❖ ❖

As Barbara Mandrell sang, "I was country when country wasn't cool," my brother was an Atlanta Braves fan before they became America's team and began winning pennants. He had a nice yellow Buick Regal, and his South Carolina-issued license plate read, "BRAVES."

After being college sweethearts at Clemson, he proposed to my now sister-in-law and persuaded her to spend a portion of their honeymoon at the Braves' spring training camp in Florida! Ah, the wonders of young love!

When they arrived at the stadium and had settled into their seats, the announcer came over the P.A. system to "Welcome newlyweds Mr. and Mrs. Frank Hammond" to the game. The woman seated next to my sister-in-law turned to her incredulously and said, "What kind of son-of-a-bitch would bring his new wife to a Braves game on their honeymoon?"

My sister-in-law smiled and offered to introduce her to the SOB!

Despite having been raised taking golf lessons at the country club, attending private school, and being a member of Kappa Alpha, my brother developed a love for NASCAR. He would rent an RV, load the family up, and head to Bristol, Darlington, or wherever the next race was being held. He had all the racing regalia, including a cooler packed with PBR beer. My family was amazed by his conversion to a pseudo-redneck.

One summer evening, we gathered at my parents' house for a family dinner. One of the attendees was my eight-year-old nephew, my brother's son. While the men were grilling burgers, my nephew complained to me that while his family was vacationing at the beach, his daddy wouldn't allow him or his younger sister to watch television. I told him about a similar situation that had occurred in Columbia. Some friends of mine had told their children that if they would refrain from watching any TV during the school year (except the news), they would be rewarded by selecting a family trip to anywhere in the world. The children of the Columbia couple held up their end of the bargain, and when school was dismissed in May, they chose to go on a safari to Africa. I encouraged my nephew to strike this same deal with his father: if he and his younger sister didn't watch TV all summer, they could choose a family vacation anywhere in the world.

His eyes lit up, and I could almost hear the

wheels turning in his head. I queried him as to which exotic locale he would choose to visit with his family. He immediately replied, "DAYTONA MOTOR SPEEDWAY!!!" I shook my head and decided that it would be up to me to elevate his desires and show him the true wonders of the world.

My parents were blessed with six grandchildren—three granddaughters and three grandsons, one of whom is the above-mentioned child of my brother. I have a son also, as does my sister. On another occasion at my parents' house, my mother had gathered the three grandsons around her to regale them with some tale. As she surveyed the three of them, she turned to my brother's son and told him he was her third favorite grandson! Number three out of three! No rhyme, reason, or rationale for this. Thankfully, it is something they have laughed about for years!

Chapter 23

Friends For Life

My father was a diplomat with the patience of Job. If patience is considered a virtue, he was the most virtuous man I've ever known. And it took every ounce of patience he had to live with my capricious mother for over fifty years! Daddy was wonderful, witty, charming, and managed to surround himself with lifelong friends who possessed these same qualities.

One such friend was the local Cadillac dealer, Bobby Joe Collins. He and Daddy had known each other since childhood, and his nickname for my father was "Skin," because of his tall lanky frame. They ate lunch together often and were at a local downtown restaurant one day when Bobby Joe observed the family dynamics at a nearby table. This was a large group with the matriarch presiding over everyone. Her children and grandchildren were extremely solicitous of her, showering her with attention and affection. Bobby Joe turned to my father and made a very astute observation:

"Skin, you see that old woman at that table and how her children are fawning all over her? Well, you can bet she still has all her money, because if she had already given them their inheritance, she'd be in a nursing home, screaming, 'Water! Water!' and not out dining in a fancy restaurant."

This proved to be prophetic, and my parents heeded this advice until their deaths, after which we received our inheritance.

Another old family friend, Billy Frazier, suffered a stroke, and EMS had to be summoned to his house. As Billy was being carried out on a stretcher, the medical technician asked him if he was allergic to anything.

He beckoned to the tech to come closer and he whispered in his ear, "I'm allergic to mean women."

When I moved to Columbia, my father and I talked on the telephone a couple of times a week. He would catch me up on all the Greenville news. As he aged, much of the conversation centered on their friends who were in failing health. Bubba and Suzanne Reynolds were two of my parents' best friends, and Bubba had been suffering for years from a variety of illnesses. During one chat with my father, Daddy told me that Bubba was losing his battle with cancer, and they had called in hospice. We went on to discuss other things, and before he hung up, I asked him what he and Momma were doing for the weekend. He replied, "Well, Saturday night we're going to have dinner at The Poinsett Club with the Reynolds."

I said, "Daddy, I thought they had called in hospice for Bubba?"

He said, "Well, they have, but he still has to eat!"

Love that attitude!

Caroline Stephenson

Along with their many friends, my parents commandeered bars at The Pontevedra Beach Club, walked the boroughs of New York, hiked the Rockies, and sailed the Caribbean Islands. While drinking one night on the island of Bimini in the late 1960s, activist and Congressman Adam Clayton Powell strode up to their table and told them to "Keep the faith, Baby!" They interpreted this as Bacchus would have and continued to eat, drink, and be merry for the next fifty years. And they did, with gusto!

Chapter 24

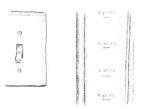

Growing Up

My childhood years, teens, and early twenties were pretty idyllic, and I saw no need to give up all the fun to take the sobering steps required to mature into adulthood. After all, when I was young, my maternal grandparents who doted on me lived only a short bicycle ride away, and my father kept my mother's volatile nature somewhat in check. Next came high school and college, which were a whirlwind of fun. It was only after I finished college that I began to look beyond the next party, the next vacation, and the next boyfriend. I consciously made a decision that it was time for me to grow up.

I got married at twenty-seven, had a career, bought a house, and purchased a car. My life seemed to be moving along swimmingly, and I felt like I had become a full-fledged adult. The next event in the world of adulthood was the birth of my first child, Callie, which changed everything. She wasn't hitting her milestones as early as other children her age. After I raised this with her pediatrician, we began a battery of genetic testing, aptitude tests, and further doctor consultations, none of which revealed why she wasn't performing on the same level as other children her age. I enrolled her in occupational therapy, speech therapy, and a school for children who learn differently. She continued to progress, but never could quite catch up to her peers.

During this time, my grandmother was a constant force in my life. She took a special interest in Callie, and I was thankful for her steadfastness. She was as involved with both of my children as my mother was uninvolved. When my children were born, my mother came up with a set of requirements they had to meet before she would invite them to spend the night at her house. The first rule was that they must sleep through the night. Once that was achieved, a new requirement would be added—when they could walk, when they were potty trained, when they no longer needed a car seat. The list went on and on. In my memory, the only time my children ever spent the night with my parents without me being present was when I attended a mandatory weekend-long educational seminar and was unable to find a babysitter.

By the time my second child, Hal, was born, my husband had become as absent as my mother. My father was deeply distressed about my husband's attitude toward us and hired a private detective, who quickly discovered his adultery. Left with two small children to raise as a single mother, I felt like I had entered a whole new level of adulthood and all the responsibility that came with it. Though my mother was not present physically, she was always ready to give me her opinions on raising children, albeit from a distance. Despite her lack of maternal instinct, she gave me three pieces of advice that I heeded; they proved to be invaluable:

1. Your children are only little for a short time so be sure to enjoy them.
2. You have your brains, your health, and your looks. There is nothing you are incapable of achieving.

3. You are the parent. Your children have lots of friends, but you aren't one of them. However, if you parent correctly, you will have the opportunity to be their friends one day, just not now.

I wish the mother capable of uttering those words had been there for me—to prop me up and keep me from falling. But with the help of my grandmother and my friends, I made it through the tough times. I remarried, and my children and I grew up.

Callie was able to overcome many of her limitations and leads an active and independent life in Columbia. Her drive, sense of humor, and joie de vivre make her a pleasure to be around. Her brother has grown into a responsible and caring adult with a great future ahead of him. In retrospect, Callie helped us all to be better people by showing us how to persevere, see the best in others, and choose to live a happy life. The three of us grew up together, and now we are all adults. And just as my mother predicted, we are all friends.

Chapter 25

Here Comes The Judge

Good friends are there for you during good times and bad. If you could name all the perfect qualities in a friend, they would be embodied in Holly Pearson Carlisle. One of the luckiest days of my life was in 1987, when having resigned from my job after having my first child, I joined a tennis team and met Holly. She related a mishap that had occurred over the previous weekend. She and a friend had gotten locked out of her house on a well-traveled street in Columbia's Heathwood neighborhood. She remembered she had left the window over the front door unlocked. The next step was to get a ladder, climb up to the second story, and go in through the window. Holly made it up the ladder, but got stuck climbing headfirst into the window with her backside on full view to the passing pedestrians and motorists.

At that moment, I just knew I had to be her best friend! She is now my partner in crime, my real estate advisor, my bridge and tennis partner, and the best damn friend in the whole wide world.

Once, after a fierce game of tennis at the country club, we decided we had a little energy left to take a walk. When we had gone two miles, Holly stopped and announced she could go no further. Her reason— her thighs were rubbing together and giving her a rash! I inquired how she thought we were going to get back to the club, and she explained we were going to hitchhike. She pointed out that with my long, tanned legs and short tennis skirt, we were sure to get a ride! Well, sure enough, a plumber stopped, we hopped in atop his pipes and gaskets, and he delivered us back to the tennis courts.

During the dark days of my divorce, Holly was always devising a new adventure to distract me from my troubles. One of her plans involved the warring tenants at a quadraplex she owned and rented. It seemed two of the residents, Josephine and Jeanette, were at each other's throats. The two had formerly been best friends until Josephine got a mutt from the pound named Brownie. That's when the trouble began. Josephine adored Brownie, whom she called a "continental" dog (whatever in the hell that meant!), and Jeanette was extremely jealous. No longer did the two share boxes of Kentucky Fried Chicken or take evening strolls together. Brownie had replaced Jeanette as Josephine's best friend. It got so bad that when Brownie would poop in the quadraplex's yard, Jeanette would dash out of her apartment, circle the poop with grits, and call Animal Control as a way of getting back at Josephine for forsaking her for Brownie. The situation had deteriorated into all-out warfare, resulting in Holly receiving dozens of calls a day from Jeanette complaining about Brownie.

Finally, Holly had had enough! She called and asked me if I would act as a judge to settle the dispute between the two tenants once and for all. The plan sounded like an interesting diversion from dealing with all the headaches of my divorce, so I agreed. Holly had told her tenants she was bringing a judge (that would be me!) over to listen to their complaints, and had secured a promise from them that they would abide by the judge's ruling and stop the constant calling. Holly picked me up with judge's robes and accoutrements in her back seat. My wardrobe consisted of a choir robe, reading glasses, a gavel, and a stack of encyclopedias.

Upon arrival at the complex, we noticed the tenants had moved the kitchen table to the front yard and placed a chair behind it to serve as my bench. The arguments began with the goal of bringing peace to the quadraplex and the cessation of calls to Holly. As an impartial justice, I listened to the testimony from both sides and ruled that there was enough room in Josephine's life for Brownie and Jeanette. Thinking the issue was resolved, I picked up my gavel and thick books and headed to the car, but Jeanette was right on my heels. Unbeknownst to me, Holly had told Jeanette that before I became a judge (haha!), I had been a patent lawyer.

Well, it seems I was just what Jeanette had been searching for. She told me she wanted to hire me to sue Kimberly Clark, because she had invented the pinless diaper before they had, but they had received the patent for it. Lord help me! The end result of all of this was Jeanette began calling me dozens of times a day, while Holly's phone remained silent! I finally told Jeanette I had retired from the legal profession, and the calls ceased.

With Holly by my side, we've been able to talk our way past guard gates, assume new identities, go coon hunting, canoe down wild rivers, and renovate houses—she even hosted my second wedding! I don't think there's anything I can't do with her by my side. If I hadn't met Holly, I'd have missed all the fun!

Chapter 26

The Blow Job

I have a friend who is beautiful and smart but still rather naïve, even into her fifties, despite having been married for thirty years. Several of my girlfriends had planned a tennis weekend on Hilton Head Island and the "innocent" one was included. We had just settled into a booth for lunch at Charlie's L'Etoile Verte when this particular friend posed the following question to the rest of us:

"Has anyone at this table ever given someone a blow job?"

WHAT?!? We were all dumbstruck and lost our

ability to speak.

She then continued, "I mean I just do not understand how a man could enjoy having his fanny cheeks spread apart and someone blowing into his heinie hole."

That comment sent us all into wild laughter, rolling onto the floor. When we regained our composure, one of our "wiser" friends took it upon herself to enlighten our ingenue about what a blow job really is. Once the true meaning of this act penetrated her pretty little head, she commented:

"Ooooh, I may have done that once or twice!"

God deliver us all!

Chapter 27

My Darling Great Aunt

My great aunt Maude, on my father's side of the family— by far the saner side—was quite a character. Maude had many husbands, but no children, which left her to indulge her great-nieces and her dogs. It was the Christmas of 1957, and I was four years old and gaga over horses and dress-up clothes. Maude arrived at our house with presents galore for my baby sister and me. When I tore the wrapping off my gift and opened it, I found an authentic cowgirl outfit. It was red, trimmed in white leather, with guns and boots to match. I fell instantly in love with Maude.

At the time of her marriage to her third husband, Dr. Jervey, she had a little Pomeranian named Pap. He (and I mean the dog, not Dr. Jervey), was the love of her life. Dr. Jervey was a staid older gentleman, and Pap was a lively, barky young dog. Several months into their marriage, Dr. Jervey had had just about enough of Pap. He told Maude, "Either that dog goes or I do!" Maude calmly turned to Dr. J. and told him that Pap had been around a lot longer than he had and wasn't going anywhere. Realizing his empty threat, he left the room to refill Pap's water bowl and get himself a stiff drink.

Unfortunately, at a relatively young age, Maude suffered a debilitating stroke to which she later succumbed. Her house was sold, and it fell to my mother to clean out her pantry. My mother accepted this task with relish because at Christ School we had weekly food drives for the poor, and my mother was constantly going to the Winn-Dixie to buy soup and peas. Maude's pantry would save her from this chore. Maude was well-traveled and had a sophisticated palate. Instead of the usual cans of beans and tomatoes, her pantry was filled with such exotic items as Welsh Rarebit, hearts of palm, and caviar. I was at the age when my greatest wish was to be exactly like my peers. Therefore it was with great trepidation that as my classmates stepped up to put their Campbell's soup, Del Monte green beans, and Amour Vienna sausages into the poor box, I deposited strange items from Aunt Maude's pantry.

Chapter 28

The End Of An Era

There have been many eras throughout history—the Prehistoric, Medieval, Renaissance—but in January 2017, one of the most turbulent eras in the realm of time ended. That was when my mother passed on to the Great Beyond. She had cut a wide path in her eighty years, leaving both wreckage and glory in her wake. For me, the moment was bittersweet. She certainly had not been warm and fuzzy, but on the other hand, she took no prisoners and spoke her mind. (Perhaps we would all have been grateful if she had spoken it a little less!)

She was charming and calculating, smart and

brash, moody and narcissistic, and suffered no fools. Her good taste was legendary. She had an innate knowledge of exactly how to pair antiques with modern pieces. She knew how to mix Pucci and Gucci and look like a model on the runway. I will always remember as she and my father headed out for a dance, her giving me a kiss and getting a whiff of her Joy perfume while her mink coat tickled my nose.

Having a mother like Joanne isn't something that I'd wish for others. However, the result of my challenging upbringing has provided me with a myriad of unique experiences. Had my life been idyllic, I would never have had the colorful stories I've written about. Turmoil makes for interesting literature, whereas peace is dull. At my mother's funeral, I found myself not so much mourning her loss, but rather longing for something I'd never had. Times when my mother could have shown support for my children and me. When she could have been there to praise me rather than criticize. To be the kind of mother who said, "I'll be there," rather than coming up with excuses why she couldn't.

Writing this book has helped me to let go of some of the disappointment I felt toward her for not being a loving and patient mother and grandmother. The kind of mother I could lean on and knew would be there to catch me should I fall. The type of mother who was encouraging and would instill in a child a sense of value that would propel her through life. However, I learned resilience, the importance of being able to think on my feet, and to stand up for myself. She had the power to charm if she so chose, but she could just as easily cut you to the quick. Not exactly the criteria for mother of the year.

At the reception following my mother's funeral, many of her friends and family were telling "Joanne" stories. One was particularly singular to my mother. At a family cookout one August, just prior to four of the six grandchildren leaving to attend Clemson, my mother summoned them to her. I thought perhaps she planned to impart some sage grandmotherly advice to the young college students. However, she began telling them that although she and my father had traveled extensively, there was one trip she had never been on that she would like for them to experience. They were imagining grandmother treating them to a voyage to the South Pacific, or perhaps a lavish European vacation. She then looked at them earnestly and told them she wanted them to take a trip on LSD!

Such was life with Joanne!

May she (and the rest of her family) rest in peace!

CPSIA information can be obtained
at www.ICGtesting.com
Printed in the USA
JSHW040311091222
34603JS00007B/19